TUNE AND REPAIR YOUR OWN PIANO

TUNE AND REPAIR YOUR OWN PIANO

A practical and theoretical guide to the
tuning of all keyboard stringed
instruments, and to the running
repair of the piano

Michael Johnson

and

Robin Mackworth-Young

HARCOURT BRACE JOVANOVICH
London and New York

Copyright © 1978 by
CLAVITUNE LTD.,
310 Edgware Road
London W2 1DY

Reprinted 1979

Library of Congress Catalog Card Number: 78 51046
ISBN: 0 15 691468 9 Pbk
ISBN: 0 15 191383 8

Printed and bound at William Clowes & Sons Limited
Beccles and London

ABCDE

CONTENTS

Part I—The Elements of Tuning

Part II—Running Repairs to the Piano

ILLUSTRATIONS

Part I
THE ELEMENTS
OF TUNING

I
INTRODUCTION

Most musicians expect to have to tune the instruments on which they play, and count the ability to do so as one of the normal and essential skills of musicianship. With some instruments, indeed, such as members of the violin family, and the trombone, the initial tuning is only part of the story, since the playing of every note is itself an act of tuning. This is not, of course, true of keyboard instruments, where the whole process of tuning must be completed before a note is played. But here the process is much more complicated, not only because of the number of notes to be tuned, but also because the relationship between the twelve notes of the scale is far from straightforward. Performers on instruments of antique type such as harpsichords and clavichords can usually do their own tuning, but many prefer to employ a professional tuner for important occasions. Pianoforte players, on the other hand, hardly ever tune their own instruments. There are several reasons why they leave the task to professionals:

(1) There are so many strings to tune – a modern pianoforte has well over 200;

(2) Setting the scale (tuning the first octave) on any keyboard instrument demands the detection and adjustment of a complicated series of fine distinctions of sound. Once this hurdle has been surmounted the process of tuning the remaining octaves is usually simple. This is not so, however, with the piano, whose unique acoustical properties make even the tuning of octaves a complex affair;

(3) The strings are set to so high a tension that the technique of adjusting them with the tuning lever demands a special skill;

(4) In temperate climates pianos hold their tune tolerably well for several months, and a few visits from a professional tuner are enough for most purposes.

So long as professional piano tuners are to be found, at a price that owners or players of pianos can afford, the present happy state of affairs can continue. But the number of tuners is diminishing, despite energetic steps to expand the intake of trainees; and their fees, like those of all skilled craftsmen, are going up. Schools and other institutions with many pianos are finding it increasingly difficult to meet the cost of regular tuning, while in some remote areas it may be almost impossible to find a tuner at all. Many piano dealers are also finding the shortage of professional tuners embarrassing. In the long run more and more pianos will have to be tuned by non-professionals if they are to be kept reasonably well in tune; and there is a need for a simple manual, written in non-technical language, to describe the basic principles and technique of the operation. That is the purpose of this book.

Happily for the non-professional, the main acoustical difficulty of tuning keyboard instruments – that of setting the scale – is a thing of the past. Those who are daunted by the description of this process in Chapter 3 can circumvent it by using a modern electronic tuning machine. For tuning the piano, however, no equipment of this kind can supersede the need for mastering the physical technique of using the tuning lever. This is described in Chapter 4.

As to the technique of tuning octaves on the piano by ear, not much can be said beyond the theoretical explanation of the so-called "stretching" of octaves given in the third and fourth sections of Chapter 2. Professional tuners simply set each string to the adjustment which gives the most acceptable sound. Those using an electronic machine should follow the instructions for each octave provided by the makers.

There are however various different kinds of tuning machine, not all of them capable of dealing accurately with the stretching of octaves. The best kind for the non-technical operator is a scientific instrument specifically designed for measuring the pitch of musical notes. The simplest and most practical of these (illustrated on page 34) gives measurements on the dial of a large electric meter.

This way of presenting the information makes the process of stretching virtually automatic and completely accurate.

2

THE PRINCIPLES OF TUNING

THE VIBRATING STRING

Surprising as it may seem, every note on a perfectly tuned piano is slightly out of tune with every other note. To see why this is so we must first consider what happens when a string is struck so as to produce a note.

At the moment of impact the string is stretched and displaced to one side. The hammer bounces back instantaneously, and makes no further contact with the string, which is then pulled back by its own elasticity towards its original position. When it reaches this position its momentum carries it further until it is stretched almost as far in the opposite direction. It then moves to and fro between these two extreme positions at a regular rate, in much the same way as a pendulum swings from side to side, only faster. To produce the A above middle C, for example, it makes no less than 440 complete (double) swings in one second. The number of swings per second – known as the frequency – can be altered in three ways, by varying (1) the weight, (2) the length, or (3) the tension of the string. The first two factors are fixed by the manufacturer of the instrument. Only the third can be altered when the instrument is in use, and this is the one used for tuning.

The vibrations of a string are not only faster than those of a pendulum, they are also more complicated. When a string is thrown into vibration the middle part, naturally, travels furthest from side to side, and the distance of travel is gradually reduced towards the ends, which are fixed. Now if the mid-point of the string is also prevented from moving (by a finger placed loosely upon it), and the string is then struck at some other point, each half-section will vibrate. By making the string vibrate in halves we have of course reduced the length of the vibrating section and so brought into play the second of the three ways of changing the frequency of the string. A string which is half as long will normally vibrate twice as fast; and the note which is produced by these vibrations will be exactly an octave higher than the original note. The diagrams at Fig. 1 show a string vibrating (a) in its full length and (b) in halves.

By placing the finger on other positions along the string we can make it vibrate in three, four, five, or more sections, causing vibrations three, four, five or more times as fast (Fig. 2 shows a string vibrating (c) in three and (d) in four sections). Vibrations which are four times as fast will (as might be expected) produce a note two octaves higher. Vibrations three or five times as fast do

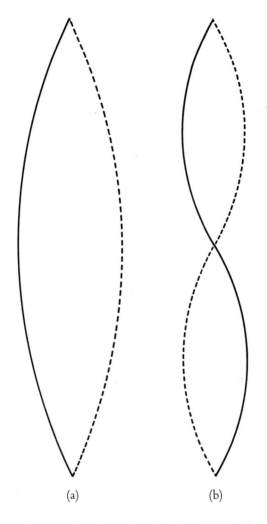

(a)　　　　　　　(b)

Fig. 1. Diagram of a string vibrating in its full length and in halves

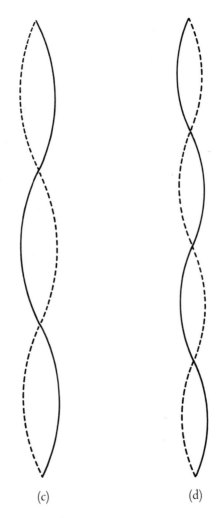

(c)   (d)

Fig. 2. Diagram of a string vibrating in three and four
       sections

something much more interesting – they produce a different note of the scale. If, for example, the full length of the string produces A, vibrations three times as fast will produce E in the octave above (i.e. an octave and a fifth higher), while vibrations five times as fast will produce the C♯ in the second octave above (i.e. two octaves and a major third higher). This is quite easy to demonstrate on the piano. The notes produced in this way by the vibrations of a string in sections or parts are known as partials (and for some purposes as harmonics or overtones). The diagram at Fig. 3 shows the notes produced by the first ten partials of the A at the bottom of the bass stave.

Now all these different ways in which a string can vibrate have been considered, for the sake of clarity, as if only one of them could happen at a time. In fact the behaviour of a vibrating string is almost unbelievably complicated, because (provided its vibrations are not impeded by anything like a finger) they all happen at once. We cannot easily visualise the appearance of a string vibrating in all these sections together, even in slow motion.

Fig. 3. Diagram of the notes produced by the first ten partials of A

But there is no need to do so. All that concerns us is a particular effect of these combined vibrations on the ear. The various vibrations – or partials – are not normally heard as separate notes, though this does sometimes happen, especially to the trained ear: but it is through them that the different notes of the scale are related to each other. Without them, indeed, there would be no harmony, and music would have no meaning. To see how this comes about, we must consider what happens when two notes of approximately the same pitch are sounded together.

If the two notes are very close to each other but not of exactly the same pitch the ear will hear only a single note which rises and falls in loudness at a regular rate. This regular rhythm, known as a "beat", gets faster if the pitch of the notes is separated, and slower if they are brought closer together. (Its speed is in fact equal to the difference between the frequencies of the two notes: so that if, for example, two strings of the A above middle C are being tuned, and one is vibrating 440 times a second, and the other 441, one beat will be heard in every second.) When the beat becomes so slow as to be imperceptible, the strings sound as a complete unity, and are said to be in tune. If the notes are now separated again the rhythm will reappear, and speed up until it forms an increasingly prominent and offensive component of the sound. When this point is reached the two notes are said to be out of tune with each other.

Now partials are simply rather weak notes, and produce beats like any other note. If therefore two piano strings which have one partial in common are struck together, and these partials are not precisely in tune, a beat will be heard between them. If the tension of one of the strings is now adjusted so as to bring them more closely into tune, the beat will slow down and eventually disappear. To take the simplest instance, if A and the E a fifth higher are simultaneously struck, the third partial (which is an octave and a fifth higher) of A will correspond to the second partial (which is an octave higher) of E. When the violinist is tuning his E string to his A string, it is to the beat between these particular partials that he listens, adjusting the tension of the E string so that the beat slows down, and continuing the adjustment until it disappears. The lower strings of the violin (D and G) are tuned in the same way, the D against the A (the common partial being the A an octave higher) and the G against the D (with the D an octave higher as the common partial).

SETTING THE SCALE

If we now transfer this process to the piano, we can extend it in both directions to the extremes of the keyboard. In doing so we should sound each of the twelve notes of the scale in turn, though some would be deep down in the bass and others high up in the treble. Our aim, of course, is to tune all the notes of the scale *within a single octave*. To make this possible we need also the ability to tune notes separated by the interval of an octave. This is in fact the easiest interval to tune, as only one partial is involved: the second partial of the lower note (produced by the string vibrating in halves) corresponds to the note produced by the whole length of the other string (which is known as the fundamental).

If that were the whole story, the process of "setting the scale" (as the tuning of the twelve notes of the central octave is known) would be scarcely more difficult than that of, say, tuning all four instruments of a string quartet. But here nature plays a trick, which anyone who cares to work out the arithmetic of the process will foresee. If we tune the central octave in rising fifths, always going upwards to the next fifth, and dropping an octave wherever necessary to keep in the middle of the keyboard, we might expect that the twelfth such operation would bring us back exactly to the original A. In fact it does not do so, but leads to a note which is significantly higher in pitch. To be exact, if the frequency of the A with which we started was 440, the A which we reach at the end of the operation will be increased to 446. This is nearly a quarter of a semitone (A♯ is 466), which is far enough out of tune to grate on the ear.

How do we get around this difficulty, and produce a scale which ends up with a note of exactly the same pitch as the one with which we began?

The answer sounds easy enough in theory but is strikingly difficult to achieve in practice – we flatten (or reduce) each fifth slightly, making exactly the same reduction to each successive interval, so that the effect is cumulative; and the amount of this reduction (which works out at about one fiftieth of a semitone, or two *cents* – a cent is a hundredth of a semitone) is so measured as to make the final A (which is of course lowered by twelve times this amount) coincide exactly with the original one. The adjustment to each fifth is so fine as to be hardly noticeable, and provided it is done accurately gives a perfectly acceptable result. It is however a highly specialised operation, which requires either prolonged training or an exceptionally gifted ear. In default of these advantages we can overcome the difficulty by using an electronic device for measuring pitch of the kind mentioned in the introduction, which enables its operator to set each note to the precise pitch required.

When the scale is set by flattening all the fifths an equal amount it is said to be equally tempered, or in equal temperament.

THE STRETCHING OF OCTAVES ON THE PIANO

We have now seen that when the scale is set in equal temperament (which is the normal tuning for a keyboard instrument, except for certain specialised purposes described later) the twelve notes are all strictly speaking out of tune with each other. But what about tuning octaves? Surely the notes bearing the same names in different octaves should all be brought exactly into tune with each other? The answer is yes for almost all instruments. The piano, however, is a notable exception, and this complicates the process of tuning it. To understand why it behaves like this we must look once more at the way in which strings vibrate.

In instruments of antique type like harpsichords and clavichords the strings are light and thin in relation to their length, and are set at a low tension. Strings of this kind can only produce a low volume of sound. The much louder sounds obtained from the piano require strings set at a far higher tension – their combined pull can amount to as much as twenty tons. An increase in tension by itself would of course increase the pitch. To compensate for this, and at the same time make the string strong enough to withstand the greater tension, it is made heavier and therefore fatter.

Now if a string is to vibrate at all it must bend, and the most abrupt part of the bending is done next to the fixed points at either end. Fat strings bend less easily than thin ones, and as the fatness is increased, so the effective point at which the vibration starts moves slightly away from either end. This makes the sounding length of the string that much shorter, and raises the pitch in proportion. So far as the fundamental (full length) vibration is concerned the effect on pitch is marginal, and reduced to insignificance by the far greater *lowering* of pitch caused by the increase in the weight of the string. If that were the only consequence the effect would not be worth mentioning; but here Nature plays another trick, which makes the relationship between the notes of a properly tuned piano different from that found in any other musical instrument; *the partials are sharpened more by the fattening of the string than the fundamental, and indeed the higher the partial the more the sharpening.*

To take a concrete example, if the tension of the A above middle C on the piano is set to give 440 vibrations per second, the half lengths of the string, which create the second partial, will vibrate at slightly more than double this frequency, namely at about 881 instead of 880. This difference represents a musical interval of one fiftieth of a semitone, or two cents. Now if the A an octave higher is set so as to sound in tune with the lower A it will be found to vibrate at 881 (because it is only at that frequency that the beat between its fundamental vibration and the second partial of the lower string will be reduced to zero). In the same way the A one octave higher still will sound in tune with A=881 when set to about 1764. The sharpening effect thus builds up from octave to octave.

At the extreme treble most tuners increase the

pitch even further. This is because these notes sound best for most purposes when matched against their namesakes two octaves lower, or even more. A match over two octaves means tuning the fundamental of the higher note to the fourth partial of the lower: and – as has already been seen – the higher the partial the greater the sharpening effect. Such a match accordingly requires even more sharpening of the higher note than if it were set to sound in perfect tune with its namesake an octave lower.

In the bass octaves of the piano, where the strings are covered (i.e. where their weight is increased by winding a second string spirally around the main string, which forms a central core) the sharpening effect is particularly marked. In the central octaves it is at its minimum and it increases again slightly as the higher octaves are reached. The effect is of course cumulative when a series of octaves is tuned across the full compass of the piano. Since, as has already been shewn, all the twelve notes of the scale are also slightly out of tune with each other, the apparently self-contradictory assertion with which this discussion began is evidently true.

TUNING THE MONOCHORDS

The notes in the bottom octave or so of the piano have only one string each. These strings, known as monochords, are exceptionally fat and heavy, and the sharpening of their partials is so marked that they present a special tuning problem. When they are tuned by ear each string is in principle tuned against its namesake an octave higher (as with all strings below the central octave when tuned in the traditional way). Now if the partials of both strings were true (i.e. not sharpened) every partial of the higher string would be matched by one of the partials of the lower string – for example the third partial of the higher string would be matched by the sixth of the lower, the fourth of the higher by the eighth of the lower, and so on, the number of the latter's partials always being double those of the former. Unfortunately the inordinate widening of the intervals between the partials which happens with monochords makes it impossible to match all the sets of partials from the two strings together at once. In fact if any one pair of partials is exactly matched all the others will be out of tune. This effect is most marked with small pianos, whose bass strings are shortest and fattest, and least so with concert grands, where they are much longer and thinner.

Now every mismatch of partials will be heard as a dissonance, and it follows that no setting of the lower string can be found at which all dissonances are eliminated. The best that the tuner can hope to do is to eliminate the most prominent single one of the dissonances. This may vary from piano to piano, and different piano-tuners may even reach different conclusions about the best setting on the same piano. In practice there are four choices: (1) the fourth partial of the lower note matched against the second of the higher; (2) the sixth of the lower against the third of the higher; (3) the eighth of the lower against the fourth of the higher; or (4) the tenth of the lower against the fifth of the higher. In terms of notes, if the note being tuned is C, the pitches of the four pairs of partials are (1) the C two octaves higher, (2) the G above that, (3) the C three octaves higher, and (4) the E above that. As a general rule the most satisfactory results are given by (2) for the lower half of the bottom octave and (3) for the higher, but the owner of a pitch measuring machine is advised to try them all out for himself, and to reach his own conclusions. Indeed he may sometimes find, where two of these settings are fairly close, that the most acceptable adjustment lies at a point midway between them.

TEMPERAMENT

A chord consists of the interaction of several notes which are sounded together. This interaction occurs when some of the partials of the lowest of these notes coincide, or nearly coincide, with the fundamentals or some of the partials of the higher notes. (The partials of the higher notes also interact between each other – but this is a subsidiary effect.) Where the coincidence is sufficiently close, these interactions are sensed as harmony; where it is less close, as dissonance.

The most harmonious of all combinations of notes is the common chord. The notes of which it is composed can be arranged in many different ways, and each arrangement evokes a different musical feeling. The arrangement which evokes the greatest sense of completion or "home" is that in which there is the greatest correspondence between the partials of the lowest note and the fundamentals of the higher ones. A good example of such an arrangement is where the three higher notes coincide with the third, fifth, and eighth partials of the lowest note.

If this chord is played (in tune – and without vibrato) by a string quartet the three higher notes will indeed correspond exactly to the appropriate partials of the lowest one, and the sound will be rich and satisfying. But if the same chord is played on a keyboard instrument tuned in equal temperament they will not do so. We have already seen that with this kind of tuning the fifths are set marginally flat, so that there will be a slight (but barely noticeable) discrepancy between the third partial of the lower G and the D. We have not yet, however, seen what happens to the interval of the major third in equal temperament tuning. Unlike the fifth, this interval is increased (or sharpened), and by a much greater amount (actually by one seventh of a semitone – or 14 cents – which is seven times as large an increase). Now if two strings which purport to be tuned to the same note but whose pitches are in fact separated by one seventh of a semitone are sounded together they will be heard as offensively out of tune. The effect is less unpleasant when one of the constituents of the sound is a partial, and still less when both are partials, as partials are very weak compared with fundamentals; but clearly the thirds and sixths of chords are going to sound much less harmonious if they are played in equal temperament than if they are played at precisely the correct pitches.

Now it is thirds and sixths which give richness to harmony, while bare fifths and fourths sound empty and austere. If fifths and fourths represent the bones of the harmonic structure, thirds and sixths are the flesh. Unfortunately we cannot bring the latter more closely into tune without putting the former out of tune by a corresponding amount. What we would gain in beauty, accordingly, we should lose in backbone.

Modifying the tuning in this way also leads to another, and more serious, disadvantage. In equal temperament tuning no interval is exactly in tune, but every interval of a particular kind (for example, every fifth) is out of tune by precisely the same amount. That is the chief virtue of equal temperament, and one which made possible the chromatic music developed during the nineteenth century. Any departure from equal temperament will destroy this uniformity. If, for instance, we alter the tuning so as to bring some of the major thirds perfectly into tune, other major thirds will be put further out of tune, and become unusable. The effect will be to enrich the harmony in some keys, while making others unplayable. Not only have we weakened the backbone, we have dislocated a vertebra. In the pure form of mean tone temperament, for example, eight major thirds are perfect, and four are unusable. Many other temperaments have been devised which represent a compromise between this extreme position and the fully chromatic qualities of equal temperament.

Historically speaking equal temperament is a newcomer. Musicians tuning their own instruments naturally tended to opt for those intervals which sounded most harmonious, and this meant bringing the most prominent partials into tune (just as the violinist does with his fifths). They found that if they went for really good tuning in some keys others were made unusable. For this reason early keyboard music is confined to a limited number of keys. Composers liked to wallow in the rich sounds of the better tuned keys while avoiding the demonic growls of the rejected ones. Music of this kind will obviously lose some of its appeal if the preferred keys are deprived of the magic of their special tuning. Many of the temperaments evolved by early composers and instrumentalists have been reconstructed by scholars, and can be directly applied to musical instruments with the aid of a pitch measuring device. Music written before the age of equal temperament can now, therefore, be heard as it was intended to be played.

In order to set up any of these temperaments with a pitch measuring device it is first necessary to find out the deviation in cents of each note of the scale from the pitch of the same note in equal temperament. Tables giving these figures for various temperaments can be found in the following books:

J. Murray Barbour: *Tuning and Temperament* (Michigan State College Press, 1953).

von Herbert Kelletat: *Zur Musikalischen Temperatur insbesondere bei Johann Sebastian Bach* (Oncken, 1960).

Pierre-Yves Asselin: *Les Tempéraments anciennes et leur Réalisation au Clavecin* (Paris, 1978).

3
SETTING THE EQUAL TEMPERED SCALE BY EAR

There are several different procedures for setting the scale, and many professional tuners have developed their own personal methods for checking the accuracy of particular notes during the process. What follows is a description of two standard methods, each with a few personal variations. The only differences between these methods is the order in which some of the notes are tuned towards the beginning of the process. Where the two methods are identical they are covered by a single description. Beginners will probably find the second method easier.

Methods 1 and 2
The first step is to tune one of the strings of middle C to a tuning fork. When tuning a string to a fork the beats for which the tuner listens can be heard most clearly when the fork is at the pitch of the string's first partial i.e. when the fork is an octave higher than the string. If the required pitch for A above middle C is 440 cycles per second, that for C an octave above middle C is 523·3.

Place a wedge between the two right hand strings of middle C on the piano. For grand pianos a felt wedge is best, while for smaller uprights a hinged device called a Papps wedge can be inserted between the shanks of the hammers. Sound the fork, and play the note so as to sound the left hand string while the fork is still vibrating. Unless the string is already exactly in tune with the fork a regular beat, or rise and fall in the volume of sound, should be heard as a result of the interaction of the two notes. If the tension of the string is adjusted in one direction or the other the speed of this beat will increase or decrease. The adjustment should be made in the direction which causes it to decrease, and should be continued until it is so slow that it has virtually stopped. The string is now in tune. (If the adjustment is continued beyond this point the beat will start up again, and increase in speed.)

Now discard the tuning fork, which is not required further. Remove the wedge and place it between the right hand string of C and the left hand string of C♯. This leaves both the middle and left hand strings of C free to vibrate. Play C and tune the middle string to the left hand string in the same way.

Now remove the wedge altogether, and tune the right hand string to the other two.

Method 1 only
Now wedge off the E above C (i.e. place a wedge

between the two right hand strings of E) and sound the left hand string together with middle C. Adjust this string until it sounds in tune with C (i.e. until the beat which can otherwise be heard when they are played together is reduced to zero). Now sharpen the E so that the beat reappears, and continue until it reaches $10\frac{1}{2}$ beats per second (most wristwatches tick 5 times a second, so there must be just over two beats per tick). Do not yet tune the middle and right hand strings of E, but leave the wedge in place.

Wedge off the G below middle C and play it against middle C. Adjust the left hand string of G until it sounds in tune, and then flatten it slightly until there is a beat of one per second.

With the wedges still in position on E and G, check these two notes together. There should be $8\frac{1}{2}$ beats per second.

Now play the triad G C E. If it sounds satisfactory tune the other strings of E and G.

Wedge off D above middle C and A below middle C.

Tune D to G, and flatten it marginally to give one beat every two seconds.

Tune A to D, and flatten it to give one beat per second.

If A is at the correct pitch, one beat every two seconds will be heard when it is played against the E which has already been tuned.

Tune the remaining strings of D and A.

Method 2 only

Now wedge off the G below middle C (i.e. place a wedge between the two right-hand strings of G) and sound the left hand string together with middle C. Adjust this string until it sounds in tune with C (i.e. until the beat which can otherwise be heard when they are played together is reduced to zero). Now flatten the G slightly until the beat reappears very slowly, and adjust it until it reaches a frequency of one per second. Do not yet tune the middle or the right hand string of G, but leave the wedge in place.

Wedge off D above middle C and A below middle C.

Tune D to G, and flatten it marginally to give one beat every two seconds.

Tune A to D, and flatten it to give one beat per second.

Leaving the wedges in position on A, D, and G, wedge off E, tune it to A, and flatten it to give one beat per two seconds. Now play E and C together. If E is at the correct pitch there should be a fast beat at the rate of $10\frac{1}{2}$ per second (most watches tick five times a second, so there should be just over two beats per tick). If there are too many beats the E will be sharp, and if too few, it will be flat. Correct the pitch of E accordingly, and adjust A, D, and G as necessary. Then play the triad G C E. If this sounds satisfactory, tune the remaining strings of G, D, A, and E.

Methods 1 and 2

Wedge off the B and F♯ below middle C.

Tune B to E one beat per second flat.

Check the setting of B by playing the major third G–B; the number of beats per second should be marginally less than that given by the major sixth G–E.

Tune F♯ to B one beat per second flat.

Check this setting by playing the minor third F♯–A, which should give a beat of $10\frac{1}{2}$ per second, the same speed as is given by the major third C–E, with which it can be compared.

Tune the remaining strings of B and F♯.

Wedge off C♯ above middle C and G♯ below middle C.

Tune C♯ to F♯ one beat per two seconds flat.

Check this by playing the major third A–C♯, which should give a beat fractionally faster than the third G–B already tuned.

Tune G♯ to C♯ one beat per second flat.

Check this by playing the major third G♯–C. The beat should be slightly faster than that of the third G–B, and slightly slower than that of the third A–C♯. (The speed of the beats given by major thirds goes up half a beat per second with each successive higher third: e.g. G–B=8, G♯–C=$8\frac{1}{2}$, A–C♯=9 etc.)

Tune the remaining strings of G♯ and C♯.

Wedge off D♯ above middle C and A♯ below middle C.

Tune D♯ to G♯ one beat per two seconds flat.

Check this by playing the major third B–D♯, which should give 10 beats per second ($\frac{1}{2}$ a beat per second slower than the third C–E).

Make a further check by playing the major sixth F♯–D♯. This should give a beat of 8 per second, half a beat per second slower than the sixth G–E, which was played when tuning the first triad.

Tune A♯ to D♯ one beat per second flat.

Check this by playing the major third A♯–D. The speed of the beat should fall between those of the thirds A–C♯ and B–D♯. In addition the third F♯–A♯ should give half a beat per second less than the third G–B.

Tune the remaining strings of D♯ and A♯.

Wedge off the F above middle C and the F below middle C.

Tune the upper F to A♯ one beat per two seconds flat.

Check this by playing the fourth C–F. This should give one beat per second.

Tune the lower F to the higher F.

Check this by playing the third F–A. This should produce 7 beats per second, half a beat less than the third F♯–A♯.

Check again by playing the major sixth F–D. This should produce $7\frac{1}{2}$ beats per second, half a beat less than the sixth F♯–D♯.

Tune the remaining strings of both Fs.

The scale is now set from F to F.

4

THE TECHNIQUE OF USING THE TUNING CRANK ON THE PIANO

GENERAL

The secret of keeping a piano really well in tune is to tune it often. The shorter the interval between tunings the smaller the adjustments which have to be made, and large adjustments are to be avoided because they set up powerful stresses in the frame of the piano. These lead to further gradual movement in the strings, which put them once more out of tune. Since the combined pull of all the strings on the frame may approach 20 tons the forces at work are considerable. But the same forces which make it necessary to avoid massive adjustments to individual strings also make it difficult to achieve fine ones, because when a string is under high tension the wrest pin by which it is both secured and adjusted tends to move in jerks. Even if the pin is successfully moved to the correct position, moreover, it will not hold that position for long unless it is correctly "set". A special lever, which calls for a special technique, is used to manipulate it. Once mastered, the application of this technique at frequent intervals will keep the instrument in far better tune than if it is visited only three or four times a year by a professional tuner, however skilled.

THE TECHNIQUE OF FINE TUNING

Each string should always be tuned marginally sharp at first, and then eased to the right pitch by gentle flattening. To achieve this movement with full control, the following technique should be used.

(1) Grand Pianos

Place the tuning crank on the wrest pin of the string to be tuned, with the handle pointing to the right of the pin and slightly forward (i.e. in the direction corresponding to 2 o'clock on the clock face, looking down on the piano from above).

Now place the ball of the right hand (i.e. the underneath of the knuckles) on the handle with the little finger hooked round the handle at the end, and the other three fingers loosely extended (i.e. *not* hooked around it). The thumb should extend to the left and press gently forward against the handle, in a direction away from the wrist (see illustration at Fig. 4).

To raise the pitch slightly, press the thumb forward, grip the handle with all four fingers, and jerk it backwards and very slightly upwards pulling it a little towards a point just above the treble end of the piano.

Fig. 4. Using the tuning crank on grand pianos

To lower the pitch slightly, release the three middle fingers, leaving only the little finger hooked around the handle. Now press gently with the ball of the hand and with the thumb forward and very slightly downward towards the strings of the piano (the downwards movement must not be exaggerated and should be more in the mind than in the action). On getting close to the correct position stop thinking consciously about turning the pin, and continue to press gently in the same direction until the right setting is reached.

Once this technique has been mastered adjustments of as little as one cent can be made quite easily with the help of a pitch measuring device. (See Fig. 5.)

(2) Upright Pianos

The technique is the same as with grand pianos, except that the direction in which the handle of the crank is pushed or pulled is changed to accord with the horizontal position of the wrest pin.

There is more than one possible position for the crank. Perhaps the most satisfactory is with the

Fig. 5. An electronic instrument for measuring the pitch of
       musical notes

handle pointing upwards and to the left, in the
direction corresponding to 10 o'clock on the clock
face. The wrist should be placed to the right of the
handle (looking from the front) with the thumb in
front of it, i.e. between it and the eyes, and the
index finger on top of it (see illustration at Fig. 6).

To raise the pitch slightly, hook the three middle
fingers round the handle and pull towards the far
right hand top corner of the piano, i.e. to the right
and slightly inwards towards the strings of the
piano.

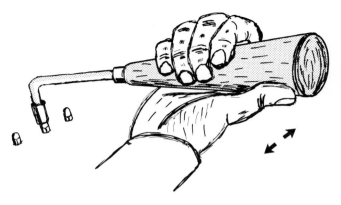

Fig. 6. Using the tuning crank on upright pianos

To flatten the pitch slightly, release the three middle fingers and press gently with the index finger on top of the handle, guiding the hand with the thumb on one side of the handle and the fingers on the other. For the final adjustment, which "sets" the pin, tap the end of the handle with the index finger towards the bass key block and a little outwards. The final movement is felt much more as the application of thought than as a physical effort to bend the pin. In fact, the minimum of physical force is required, and there should on the contrary be a sense of relaxation.

Part II
RUNNING REPAIRS
TO THE PIANO

5
INTRODUCTION

The piano is an intricate and precisely engineered mechanism with several hundred moving parts. The layman can no more expect to carry out major repairs upon it than he could upon his motor car. Just as with the motor car, however, there are a few simple running repairs which most owners can learn to do without putting the mechanism to undue risk: and there are other more complicated ones, comparable to those which patrolmen of motoring organisations like the AA and RAC in Britain or the AAA in the United States can carry out on cars, which anyone with a modest talent as a handyman can learn to do for himself. It is with these last two kinds of repair that this section of the book is concerned.

Even for these kinds of repair, however, the layman will be well advised, if there is any choice, to call in a professional. Every piano tuner is trained to do running repairs up to the patrolman degree of complexity and a few, who have served an apprenticeship with a firm of piano manufacturers, are qualified to carry out more fundamental repairs. Some repairs, moreover, call for special tools which piano tuners carry with them but which the ordinary householder will not possess.

This said, the fact remains that professional help is not always available, especially in remote areas: and if, for example, one or two notes of an instrument are not functioning properly, a few elementary repairs carried out either by the owner or by a neighbour who is handy with household tools may make all the difference between a piano that is in acceptable order and one that is unplayable. Even so, no layman should attempt any repair whatever to the action of the piano without instruction of the kind contained in this chapter. A false move may easily lead to damage which can be rectified only at great cost, and may prove irreparable if the instrument cannot be returned to the factory.

In dealing with the mechanism of the piano, therefore, it is always best to err on the side of caution, and to use professional help wherever this is to be found. Even where help is at hand, however, the pianist to whom the information in the following pages is new may still find advantage in exploring them. They will at least indicate ways in which he can take greater care of the delicate and complicated instrument on which he plays: and it is not impossible that they may also help him to make better use of the refinements of its mechanism, and so to improve his touch.

6

GENERAL DESCRIPTION OF THE ACTION

There is a fundamental difference between the actions of upright and of grand pianos, but this apart the actions in different makes of piano are broadly similar. Those described in the following pages are typical of the majority of instruments.

UPRIGHT PIANOS

The various parts of the action which belong to a single note are shown in their working positions in Fig. 7. These parts consist basically of three separate moving assemblies mounted on a wooden beam, sometimes strengthened by a metal covering, which runs the full width of the piano, and on which the actions for all the other notes on the instrument are mounted as well. This beam is known as the *butt rail*, and is shown in cross section on the diagram as no. 1. Each of the three assemblies is secured to the butt rail by a flange (2, 7, 28), whose function is to provide a pivot on which the assembly concerned can turn.

The first or lowest assembly is that of the lever,

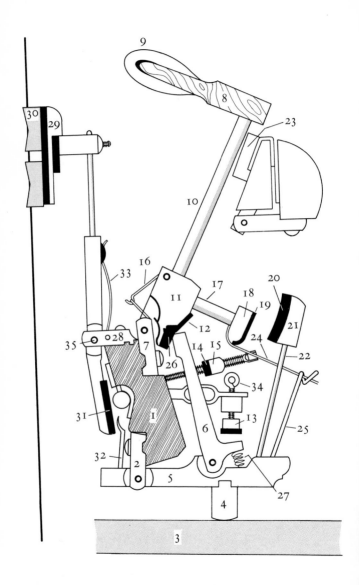

Fig. 7. The upright action

1. Butt rail
2. Lever flange
3. Key
4. Lever body heel
5. Lever body
6. Lever jack
7. Butt flange
8. Hammer head
9. Hammer felt
10. Hammer shank
11. Butt
12. Butt cover or notch (doeskin)
13. Escapement button
14. Check rail cover
15. Check rail
16. Butt spring
17. Balance hammer shank
18. Balance hammer head
19. Balance hammer cover (leather)
20. Check felt (hard felt)
21. Check
22. Check wire
23. Hammer rest rail
24. Tape tie
25. Tie or bridle wire
26. Butt cushion
27. Jack spring
28. Damper flange
29. Damper head
30. Damper felt
31. Damper stem covering
32. Damper spoon
33. Damper spring
34. Escapement rail screw
35. Damper bearing

which transfers movement from the key into the action. The movement starts of course when the pianist depresses the front part of the key. This raises the back part (3), which pushes up the small projection or heel (4) on the underneath of the lever body (5). Now the lever body is pivoted on the lever flange (2) which is fixed to the butt rail. As the outer part of the lever body moves upwards it carries with it the lever jack (6). This imparts movement to the second assembly.

The second assembly is that of the hammer. It is pivoted on the butt flange (7) which is also fixed to the butt rail. It consists basically of the hammer head (8) and associated felt (9), mounted on a long thin shank (10), terminating at its foot in a specially shaped protuberance known as the butt (11). The purpose of the butt is to provide a surface against which the lever jack (6) can act as it rises. As it is forced upwards it presses against the bottom of the butt, through a protective covering of doe-skin (12), and swings it upwards on its pivot, so that the hammer is thrown towards the string.

The movement which leads to the hammer striking the string is thus conveyed in three stages, through (a) the key (b) the lever assembly and (c) the hammer assembly. This may seem an unnecessarily complicated arrangement, but is indispensable for three reasons. First, the hammer must not be held against the string when the key is fully depressed, otherwise it will stifle the vibrations. On the contrary, it must be free to rebound even when the key is held down. Second, when the hammer has rebounded it must not bounce back again so as to strike the string a second time. Third, it must nevertheless strike once more as soon as the key is partially released and again depressed.

These three requirements are met by the mechanism known as the escapement. This is how it works. The lever jack (6) has a projection on the side. As the top of the jack moves upwards, carrying the butt with it and swinging the hammer towards the string, this projection collides with a stationary obstacle in the shape of the escapement button (13), which does not move because it is fixed to the butt rail. Now the lever jack is joined to the lever body (5) by a pivot: and the effect of the collision with the button is to turn the jack sideways on this pivot so that it moves out of the range of the returning butt. (The distance through which it travels is limited by the felt cover (14) of the check rail (15). This, like the butt rail to which it is fixed, runs right across the piano.) When the hammer bounces back, therefore – assisted when travelling slowly by the butt spring (16) – the butt does not hit the top of the lever jack (if it did it would rebound onto the string). Instead its motion is arrested by another part of the mechanism, specially devised to prevent a rebound. Fixed to the side of the butt by a shank (17) is a small wooden block (18) known as the balance hammer head, covered with leather (19) on the far side. As this comes down it is caught sideways on by a piece of thick felt (20) mounted on a wooden support called the check (21), which is fixed to the lever body by a wire (22) which can be bent. The felt, which rises and comes forward with the end of the lever body when the key is depressed, acts as a brake, and brings the motion of the hammer assembly to a halt. When the key is released, and the lever body (5) falls, the felt drops away, and the hammer is free to fall further, until brought to a final halt by the hammer rest rail (23). (This, like the butt rail, runs right across the piano.) The last stage of the balance hammer head's descent is speeded up by a tug from a piece of tape which is fixed to it – the tape tie (24). This is pulled down by the falling lever body through an adjustable wire (25). Meanwhile the projection on the lever jack (6) is no longer held against the button and the jack is forced back to its original position against the butt cushion (26) by the jack spring (27), so that if the key is depressed again it will once more push against the butt, and cause the hammer to strike.

There remains the third assembly, which is concerned with damping. This consists of a long arm pivoted on the damper flange (28), (which like the other flanges is fixed to the butt rail) terminating in the damper head (29) and its associated felt (30) at the upper end. The lower end has a covering (31) to protect it from an arm called the damper spoon (32) which projects from the back end of the lever body (5). When the key is depressed, and the front end of the lever body is raised, this arm pushes against the lower end of the damper assembly, causing the damper felt to come away from the string. When the key is released, the damper spoon retreats and the damper felt is pushed back against the string by the damper spring (33).

It is obvious that the complicated mechanism of the complete action depends for its proper working on the free movement of its bearings and the efficiency of its springs. Most of the faults which afflict it arise from failure in one or other of these.

GRAND PIANOS

The action in grand pianos (Fig. 8) is simpler than in uprights, because it relies more on gravity and less on springs and ties. Indeed there is only one spring in the mechanism – the lever spring (1), which is much more robust than any of the springs in the upright action, and so less liable to fail.

When the key is depressed its back part (2) is raised, and with it the capstan screw (3) which is adjustable. This pushes the lever heel (4) upwards, and with it the main part of the action known as the *lever body* (5). This is pivoted on the lever flange (6), which is screwed to a fixed beam running across the width of the piano known as the lever rail (7). As the lever body swings upwards on its pivot, the lever jack (8) is pushed upwards through

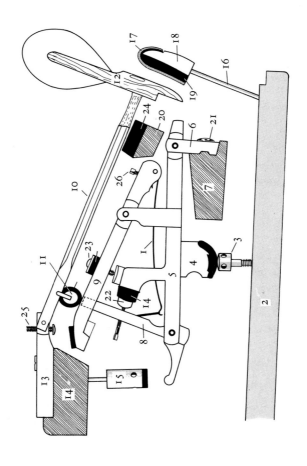

Fig. 8. The grand action

1. Lever spring
2. Key
3. Capstan screw
4. Lever heel
5. Lever body
6. Lever flange
7. Lever rail
8. Lever jack
9. Repetition rail
10. Hammer shank
11. Hammer shank roller
12. Hammer head
13. Hammer shank flange
14. Hammer rail
15. Escapement dolly
16. Check wire
17. Check leather (doeskin)
18. Check
19. Check underpad (felt or cloth)
20. Hammer rest rail
21. Flange screw
22. Jack regulating button
23. Repetition rail regulating screw
24. Hammer rest cushion
25. Drop screw or grand set-off screw
26. Grub screw

a slot (not visible in the diagram) in the repetition rail (9) onto a soft projection on the shank (10) of the hammer assembly known as the *hammer shank roller* (11), which it pushes upwards in turn. This launches the hammer (12) upwards on its pivot (which is fixed by a flange (13) to a second fixed beam, also running across the width of the piano, called the *hammer rail* (14)) so that it strikes the string.

Once the hammer has struck the string it falls downwards: and if the top of the lever jack were still in the same place the hammer shank roller would bounce off it, and cause the hammer to strike the string again. An escapement mechanism is therefore provided, as with the upright action, to move the lever jack out of the way. As the lever jack rises, a long projection at its foot collides with a small cylindrically shaped obstacle called the *escapement dolly* (15). This collision swings the lever jack on its pivot so that the upper end slides to one side of the hammer shank roller (the slot in the rocker which conceals the top of the lever jack from view in the diagram is wide enough to permit this). As with the upright action, the return motion of the hammer is now arrested by another mechanism which prevents a rebound. A thick wire (16) fixed to the back end of the key carries an assembly shaped like a small brake shoe, with a surface of doeskin (17) on a base of wood (18) surmounted by felt or cloth (19). This is called the *check*. As the front of the key is depressed, the back rises, and swings the check upwards and towards the path of the returning hammer, which it meets sideways on so as to bring it to a halt.

As the key is released the check falls away, but the hammer is prevented from falling with it by the repetition rail (9) which supports the hammer shank roller (11). There is nothing, however, to prevent the lever body (5) from falling, and as it does so the projecting base of the lever jack (8) comes away from the escapement dolly (15), so that the lever jack is free to return to its original position. It is pulled back into this position by the lever spring (1). This spring serves a double purpose, as it also forces the top end of the repetition rail (9) upwards, and lifts the hammer shank roller (11) so that the lever jack can slip under it. The note can now be struck again.

The functioning of the damper mechanism (unlike that of upright pianos) is simple and there is no need to describe it.

7

REMOVING AND REPLACING THE ACTION

Some of the repairs described in the following pages can only be carried out if the action is first removed from the piano. Before starting to remove it, clear a flat surface on which to place it when it has been removed. Not only is it heavy but it also takes up a lot of room, and may be damaged if placed on top of loose objects, or even if placed on a surface which is not perfectly flat. In either case the resultant damage to grand actions may be particularly serious, as the key frame may twist, and impair the smooth working and regularity of the action. The only cure for this condition is to replane the underside of the key frame to fit the key bed, an operation which demands a high degree of professional skill.

UPRIGHT PIANOS

To remove the action
Open the top, remove the front panel and the keyboard lid.

The action is usually held to the frame of the

piano by two brass buttons or knurled knobs each of which is screwed onto a threaded post. Unscrew them. Place both hands on the rail against which the hammers rest when not in action (the hammer rest rail) and pull it gently away from the strings, until the metal framework which contains the action comes clear of the threaded posts to which it has been secured. Lift the whole assembly carefully away from the piano and place it on the prepared surface.

To replace the action

Each of the upright members of the frame which contains the action (called the "action standards") has a cast ball or other locating device underneath. These balls fit into hemispherical or other suitably shaped sockets on the part of the piano frame which lies immediately underneath the keyboard (called the "key bed"). Lift the action by the hammer rest rail, locate the cast balls into the sockets, and tilt the frame of the action back towards the strings until the threaded posts protrude through the holes in the action standards. Replace the buttons.

GRAND PIANOS

To remove the action

Remove the keyboard lid (which is known as the fall).

Beyond each end of the keyboard, and separating it from the side of the piano, is a wooden block, called a *key block*. Each of the two blocks is held in position by a single large screw whose head can be seen from underneath the piano. Unscrew and remove the screw, and then remove the blocks.

In front of the keyboard is a long wooden strip, called the *lock front*, also held in position by screws accessible from underneath. Remove these screws, and then remove the strip.

The frame of the action is now free to slide out of the piano horizontally. Prise it gently away from the frame of the piano, taking care not to lift it, and keeping the front of the keyboard as far as possible parallel to the front of the piano. If at first it will not budge, move one side at a time through a very small distance until both sides are free to slide together. While moving the action take care not to depress any of the keys. If a key is accidentally depressed the corresponding hammer will be raised and may catch in the frame of the piano, probably breaking the shank. When the hammers are clear of the piano frame, and before the keyboard has come out so far that it over-balances, lift the whole action and place it on the prepared surface.

To replace the action

Lift the action, place it in approximately the right position on the piano frame, and slide it gently into the piano, taking care not to depress any keys. Guides on either side will ensure that it moves to exactly the right position as it slides in. When it still has about an inch to go, depress the sustaining (loud) pedal, and keep it down until the movement is complete. The fit will seem tight because of a large spring, usually on the right, which holds the whole action to the left but permits it to shift to the right when the soft pedal is depressed.

Replace the lock front and the key blocks immediately. If the lock front is left off for any length of time subtle movements of air between the timber of the key bed and of the key frame can actually cause distortion in the latter, and make replaning necessary.

8

PROCEDURE FOR REPAIRING FAULTS

The following list describes cause and cure for many of the faults which can occur in the piano, but is not comprehensive. Some of those omitted are too obvious to need description, while others are peculiar to particular makes of piano whose mechanisms differ in certain respects from those described above. But there are few pianos and few faults to which the principles underlying these descriptions cannot be applied.

Many of the repairs described below require spare parts or materials which must be ordered from suppliers of piano components. Names of these suppliers may be obtained from piano dealers. Residents in the United Kingdom can obtain supplies from Messrs. Hecksher & Co. of 75 Bayham Street, London. N.W.1.

UPRIGHT PIANOS

Symptom 1.
A note fails to repeat rapidly.

Cause 1(a)

Either the tape tie (seen by itself in Fig. 9 and in position at no. 24 of Fig. 7), or the leather section at its end known as the tape end, has perished.

Fig. 9. The tape tie

Cure

New ties can be obtained from suppliers of piano accessories. Failing this, a replacement can be made from $\frac{1}{8}''$ linen tape, obtainable from a good quality haberdasher; and a new tape end, which is usually shaped like a spear head, but sometimes like a keyhole, can be cut from the leather of an old glove, and glued onto the tape (do not use the old tape end, even if it is intact). When the glue has dried the other end of the tape should be glued to the balance hammer head (18). The length of the tape should be the same as that of its neighbours. The hole in the tape end should then be placed over the tie wire (also called the bridle-wire (25)) and this wire so adjusted that when the soft pedal is depressed the undercarriage or lever body (5) just fails to lift. (The result of depressing the soft pedal on an upright piano is to lift all the hammer shanks so that the hammers move to a position about $\frac{5}{8}''$ nearer the strings.) When the soft pedal is raised, and provided that the key is not depressed, there should be a little slack on the tape – the same amount as on its neighbours. Too much will impair repetition.

Cause 1(b)

The butt spring (16) is broken. This spring helps the hammer to return to its resting position against gravity. Its failure does not completely inactivate the mechanism but prevents fast repetition.

Cure

A replacement for this spring must also be obtained from the supplier. The springs come in different sizes. Send the measurements of a neighbouring spring, or better still the spring itself, to the supplier.

To insert the new spring the action must first be removed from the piano. Then untie the tape (24) from the bridle wire (25) and remove the lever body (5) from the butt rail (1) by undoing the screw which secures the lever flange (2) to the butt rail. When the lever body comes away, the lever jack (6) will come with it, and this will expose the screw which secures the butt flange (7) to the butt rail. Remove this screw, and the butt (11) with the flange (7) can be taken off. The butt spring is now accessible.

The butt spring is pivoted on a short length of nylon cord, which is threaded through a hole in the top corner of the butt. To extract the faulty spring, cut the nylon cord between either side of the spring and the body of the butt with a razor blade. Remove the spring and push the ends of nylon cord out of the holes with a needle or a ladies' hair clip.

Take a new spring, which should be of the same size as its neighbours. The short end fits into a hole or groove in the butt. Place it in position, and then secure the coil by passing a nylon thread through it and the holes on either side. The gauge of the thread should be the same as, or slightly larger than, the holes. If nylon thread cannot be obtained, a temporary repair can be made by paring down a matchstick to the diameter of the holes and using this instead. It should be replaced by nylon as soon as possible as it may develop a squeak.

Cause 1(c)
One or more of the bearings may not be functioning freely.
   Cure
See chapter 9 (page 74)

Cause 1(d)
Poor regulation of either the escapement or the check.
   Cure
The escapement or set-off is regulated in upright actions by turning the escapement rail screw (also called the set-off rail button) (34). The effect of adjusting this screw is to alter the distance at which the hammer stops moving towards the string when the key is depressed so slowly that the butt (11) remains in contact with the lever jack (6). To

increase the distance rotate the screw clock-wise, and to decrease it, anticlockwise. Set the screw so that the distance for the hammer concerned is the same as for its neighbours – normally about $\frac{1}{8}''$. If the screw is so adjusted that this distance is reduced to zero the hammer will be unable to rebound when the note is playe₁ normally, and so will remain in contact with the string and block the sound.

The smooth working of the escapement can be assisted by lubricating with spirit-based blacklead that part of the butt cover (known as the *notch* – 12) which comes into contact with the top end of the jack.

If the hammer is free to rebound, and the key is depressed slowly beyond the point at which the hammer stops advancing towards the string, the hammer will then move a short distance back-wards, with the assistance of the butt spring (16) if one is provided. The point at which it stops is determined by the position of the check felt (20) which moves towards the balance hammer head as the key is depressed, and catches it sideways on with a braking action. This should be set, by bending the check wire (22), so that the hammer stops at the same distance from the string as its neighbours, normally between $\frac{3}{8}''$ and $\frac{1}{2}''$.

Regulation by the non-professional is unlikely to succeed if more than a few notes are affected, as he will find it difficult to achieve uniformity of action.

Cause 1(e)
Poor adjustment of the check rail (15).

  Cure
The check rail runs along the width of the piano, and if it is in the wrong position many or all the notes will be affected. Its function is to limit the distance which the lever jack (6) can travel away from the butt (11) when moved sideways by the mechanism of the escapement. If this distance is too short the butt cover (12) may hit the jack, and bounce off it, after the hammer rebounds from the string, so that the hammer is thrown against the string a second time. If the distance is too great the jack may take too long over the journey back to its resting position (to which it is moved by the jack spring (27) when no longer held to the side by the escapement button (13)) and rapid repetition may be impaired. To find the correct distance, make the check (21) on a few widely spaced notes inoperative by bending the check wire (22) away from the butt, and set the adjusting screws of the check rail in such a position that when the keys of these notes are depressed their hammers come to rest approximately $\frac{3}{4}''$ away from the string.

Symptom 2.
A note is silent.

Cause 2(a)
The repetition or jack spring (27) is broken. This spring causes the jack (6) to return to its operating

position when the key is raised. If it fails to function the note cannot be sounded again.

Cure

A new spring must be obtained from the supplier. These springs also come in different sizes, and the measurements of a neighbouring spring, or better still the spring itself, must be sent to the supplier. They are best removed and replaced with a pair of tweezers. To replace one, compress it with the tweezers and then insert it between the jack (6) and the lever body (5).

Cause 2(b)

One or more of the bearings has seized up.

Cure

See chapter 9 (page 74).

Cause 2(c)

The hammer shank is broken.

Cure

Remove the hammer assembly as described in 1(b) above. Extract the two parts of the broken shank by steaming the glue off the joints until it is soft. Protect the felt and leather parts of the assembly, which steam would damage beyond repair, with a covering and direct the steam away from them. Cut a new shank, obtained from the supplier, to size and secure it to the head and the butt with an animal-based glue such as Seccotine or Croid.

Symptom 3.

A damper fails to return to its string so that the string continues to sound when the key is released.

Cause 3(a)

The damper spring (33) is broken.

Cure

Remove the action from the piano.

Take a screwdriver with a spindle 8″ to 10″ long, and remove the screw which holds the damper flange (28) to the butt rail (1). The entire damper assembly will now come away from the rest of the action.

The damper spring is pivoted on a bearing pin surrounded by a sheath of nylon thread. This passes through the holes in the damper flange of which one may be seen on no. 28 of Fig. 7. Extract the faulty spring by pushing out the pin and cutting the nylon cord with a razor blade, as for the butt spring, then push out the remnants of the nylon cord.

Take a new spring of the right size (obtained from the supplier) and push the shorter end through the central hole in the damper flange. Cut this end flush with the wood. Then secure the coil with a new piece of nylon thread, followed by a bearing pin, or failing that with a pared down matchstick, as for the butt spring (see 1(c) above).

Cause 3(b)

The damper bearing (35) is not functioning freely.

Cure
See chapter 9 (page 74).

Symptom 4.
Tapping and knocking noises.

Cause 4
Wear on covers.

Cure
Wherever one wooden member of the action has contact with another, the two are separated by a layer of felt or leather. This is stuck to one of the members concerned and is called a "cover", "covering" or "cushion". Wear on any of these will make it thinner and harder, and the repeated impact of the other member against it will continue the process until that impact starts to become noisy. Parts most likely to show wear are the butt cover or notch (12 – doeskin), the butt cushion (26 – felt), the balance hammer cover (19 – leather) and the check felt (20 – hard felt).

Felts and leathers should be obtained from the supplier. After removing the parts of the action concerned as described under 1(b) or 3(a) above, cut away the worn coverings, cut the new felt or leather to shape and stick it in position.

Repairs of this kind are worth doing if only a few notes are affected: but if there is general wear on the action repair is best left to a qualified technician as the unqualified repairer is unlikely to achieve uniformity of action.

Symptom 5.
Loose action.

Cause 5(a)
Poor regulation between key and action.
  Cure
When a piano key is depressed the other end of the key, beyond the fulcrum, rises, and propels the mechanism of the action so that the hammer strikes the string. There is an arrangement for adjusting the point of contact between the key and the action. This adjustment is set so that when the key is at rest it is not only in direct contact with the action, but actually raises it slightly so that the hammer is held at a small distance above the hammer rest rail. The effect of this arrangement is that there is no lost motion between key and action when the key is depressed, while the hammer rest rail is close enough to the resting position of the hammer to absorb most of the force of its rebound when the key is released.

The mechanism of the adjustment may take several forms. Sometimes it consists of a metal capstan with holes, which may be turned by a knitting needle; sometimes of a similar capstan of wood; and sometimes of an adjustable screw under a covering of boxcloth.

The simplest way to ensure that the hammers are not being held too close to the rest rail is to hook a finger over the felt of the rest rail and pull it gently. If any hammers move back with it some adjustment is needed.

Cause 5(b)
Worn bearings.
    Cure
See chapter 9 (page 74).

Symptom 6.
Poor tone.

Cause 6
Wear on hammer heads.
    Cure
If the felt of the hammer heads (9) becomes excessively cut by the strings, the length of felt which strikes the strings gets too long, and the balance between the various partials produced by the vibrating string (which is determined by the position and length of the striking surface) is distorted. Where enough felt remains on the hammer an adequate repair can be made by removing the surface of the felt all round the hammer head with sandpaper. But if a large amount of felt has to be removed in order to reduce the length of the striking surface to normal the balance of the hammer may be upset, so that it no longer returns easily to its usual position. In addition the tone may become harsh because as the felt gets thinner so the surface gets harder. In that case the head must either be covered with new felt or be completely replaced. As recovering is done by machine the only course open to the unqualified repairer is to order a new hammer from the

supplier. The correct size can be indicated to him by drawing an outline around a neighbouring hammer on a piece of paper. If the head is set obliquely on the shank it is best to send a neighbouring head to the supplier. Failing that obtain a hammer head without a hole, and bore the hole as necessary.

If the felt has not actually been cut by the strings, but only compressed, it can be loosened, or "toned" by manipulating it with needles. This operation is also, however, best left to qualified technicians as if unskilfully done it will probably produce unevenness of tone, and may well damage the felt beyond repair. The purpose of toning is to release the tensions which have built up deep down in the heart of the felt. Fluffing up the surface may seem to produce an improvement but actually leads to a woolly sound which masks fine distinctions of tone, and ruins the touch for the sensitive player.

GRAND PIANOS

Preliminary Steps

Most parts of the grand action are inaccessible until it has been removed from the piano, and this is accordingly the first step before repairs or regulation can be started. Regulation must therefore be carried out away from the strings: and since the process involves adjustments which alter the distance of the hammer from the strings when the key is in certain positions, some substitute for the strings may be needed. A simple kind consists of a set-square one of those arms is the same length as the distance between the strings and the floor of the piano frame. This can be held with one hand so that the other arm stands over the hammer in the place of the string. A device of this kind will of course be more useful if mounted on a base so that it stands up by itself. The qualified technician uses a special jig designed for the purpose.

To extract the central part of the mechanism (called the carriage) of a particular note it is sometimes necessary to lift all the hammers and stand them on their ends, and then to lift up the whole of the hammer rest rail (Fig. 8) (20) after taking out the various retaining screws along its length. When the flange screw (21) of the carriage concerned has been removed the carriage itself can be lifted clear.

Symptom 1.
A note fails to repeat rapidly.

Cause 1(a)
Faulty bearings.
  Cure
See chapter 9 (page 74).

Cause 1(b)
Faulty regulation.

Cure

There are seven points at which the grand action is regulated, and these should be adjusted in the correct order.

(1) The jack regulating button (22) must be adjusted first as it is only accessible when the central part of the mechanism (the carriage) has been removed. Adjust it so that the jack (8) is in the same position in the slot of the repetition rail (9) as its neighbours.

(2) Replace the carriage, and adjust the repetition rail regulating screw (23) so that the top of the lever jack (8) is marginally below the top of the repetition rail (about the width of a thin card) when the hammer shank roller (11) is not resting on the repetition rail.

(3) Adjust the capstan screw (3) so that after the key has been released the hammer is in line with its neighbours (with the hammer rest rail in position the shank of the hammer should stand just clear of the felt (24) of the hammer rest rail (20)). This adjustment ensures that there is no lost motion between key and hammer when the key is first depressed.

(4) Adjust the escapement dolly or set-off screw (15) so that as the key is depressed slowly the escapement operates at the same point for this hammer as for its neighbours (if a jig to replace the string is available, the escapement should operate when the hammer is at a point about $\frac{1}{8}''$ below the string substitute).

The smooth working of the escapement can be assisted by lubricating with spirit-based blacklead that part of the hammer shank roller which comes into contact with the top end of the lever jack and with the repetition rail.

(5) Adjust the drop screw (25) which determines the height to which the repetition rail (9) can rise after the escapement has operated. At this point the repetition rail, which is itself supported by the lever spring (1) has taken over from the lever jack (8) as the support of the hammer shank roller (11). The drop screw should be adjusted so that as the key is depressed slowly beyond the point at which the escapement operates, the hammer comes to rest at the same point as its neighbours. This is normally at a distance from the string (or string substitute) of between $\frac{1}{8}''$ and $\frac{1}{16}''$.

(6) Adjust the check wire (16) so that with the key fully depressed the check leather (17) holds the hammer at the same height as its neighbours (normally between $\frac{3}{8}''$ and $\frac{1}{2}''$ below the string).

(7) Adjust the grub screw (26) which regulates the tension on the lever spring (1). To set it at the correct tension depress the key fully, so that the hammer head (12) comes to rest on the check (18). When the finger is removed lightly from the key the hammer should move slightly upwards before dropping back to rest on the rest rail.

Symptom 2.
A note is silent.

Cause 2(a)(b)
Faulty bearings or regulation.
   Cure
As for Symptom 1 above.

Cause 2(c)
Failure of lever spring.
   Cure
Obtain a new spring from the supplier. The coil of this spring is held by a bearing pin which is surrounded by a layer of bushing. Prise out the pin and cut out the cloth bushing. Insert the spring, and thread a length of nylon chord of the same width as the hole of the bearing to replace the bushing. Insert a new pin. Hitch the end of the spring onto the loop attached to the lever jack (8). (Some actions use a different type of spring which does not need a loop.) Adjust the grub screw (26) in accordance with the instructions on regulation (page 70).

Cause 2(d)
Breakage of hammer shank.
   Cure
It is sometimes possible to mend a broken shank adequately with a hard-setting glue such as araldite. Failing this a new shank must be ordered from the supplier, and in order to be certain of getting the correct size and type it is best to send him the broken one. The shank is pivoted on a normal bearing (see section on bearings page 74)

and should be fixed in place with a bearing pin. It may be necessary to broach out the bushing until the pin fits. The new shank will come complete with a new hammer shank roller. As this will be less compressed than the used one, some adjustment to the regulation will probably be necessary (see Cure 1(b) above).

Symptom 3.
Poor damping.

Cause 3(a)
Faulty damper bearings.
   Cure
On grand pianos the damper mechanism is not mounted integrally with the action, but remains within the frame of the piano when the action is removed. It is pivoted on a flange which is secured to the frame by a screw. Remove this screw and the assembly can be lifted out through the gap between the strings of the note concerned and its neighbour.

   The assembly contains two bearings. If either needs repair it should be treated in accordance with the instructions in chapter 9 (page 74).

Cause 3(b)
Poorly aligned dampers.
   Cure
Leave the damper assembly in position. Loosen

the grub screw and realign, bending the wire if necessary. Tighten the screw.

Symptom 4
Tapping and knocking noises.

Cause and Cure
As for Symptom 4 on uprights.

Symptom 5
Loose action.

Causes and Cure
As for Symptom 5 on uprights.

Symptom 6
Poor tone.

Cause and Cure
As for Symptom 6 on uprights.

9
BEARINGS

Both the upright and the grand actions each have four bearings per note, and the damping assembly on the grand has two more. If any of them fails to function freely either the striking or the damping can be affected. If they all seize up completely the action will of course stop working altogether.

Many familiar objects which have moving parts, such as motor cars, bicycles, sewing machines or lawn mowers, are made basically of metal. The bearings which support these moving parts usually consist of one metal surface sliding over another, and metal will only slide against metal if separated by a film of oil.

The piano action needs a different kind of bearing because its moving parts are made of wood, which unlike metal absorbs liquid, and cannot therefore use oil as a lubricant. In the unique kind of bearing which has been developed for the piano the place of oil has been taken by a single thin layer of a special cloth ((1) Fig. 10) surrounding a central metal pin (2) which forms the pivot. To give strength to the two wooden parts

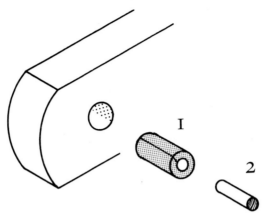

Fig. 10. A bearing

linked by the bearing one of them takes the form of a flange (see Fig. 11) whose twin arms fit on either side of a tongue projecting from the other wooden part. Each arm is provided with a hole which is lined with a layer of the special cloth. The tongue is provided with a smaller, unlined hole which is

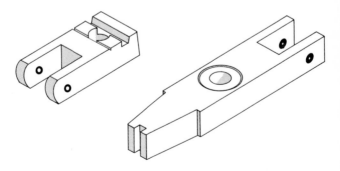

Fig. 11. Two examples of flanges

placed between the two flange holes. The metal pivot, which is threaded through all three holes, is gripped tightly by the tongue but is free to rotate in the flange.

Bearings of this kind will function for years without attention, provided that they are kept at the sort of room temperatures that are reasonably comfortable for human beings. If however they are allowed to get unusually damp, through being left either in an unheated room or in a particularly humid atmosphere, two things may happen to make them move less freely: the wood may swell and make the holes through the flange too narrow, or the bushing cloth around those holes may grow mould. The first fault can be rectified by drying the wood out, but the second calls for a skilled operation which needs a special tool and is best left to experts. When no expert is available and something must nevertheless be done if the piano is to be of any use at all, the layman may try his hand at the following procedure.

After obtaining a set of bearing pins from the supplier, push the existing pin out, taking care not to damage the bushing on the flange. This is a tricky operation, for which the professional uses a special tool, known as a decentring tool (Fig. 12). The next step demands another special tool, known as a broach. This is like a very thin round file, narrow enough to pass through the holes in the flange. If none can be obtained a substitute can be improvised by roughening another pin – which

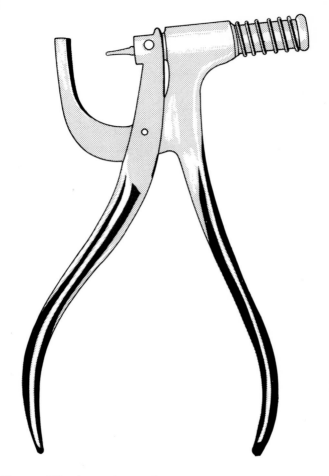

Fig. 12. The decentring tool

should be slightly thinner than the pin which has
been removed – with sandpaper. Enough of the
surface of the bushing in the flange should be
removed to permit the free passage of a new pin

one size larger than the old one (i.e. one thousandth of an inch thicker) so that it is gripped firmly but with a nice drag. The new pin must fit tightly in the unlined hole through the tongue. If it is difficult to insert into the tongue no harm will be done by assisting its progress with a touch of candlegrease.

It will be seen from this description that the operation is one of considerable delicacy. A clumsy attempt at it can easily ruin the bearing. If the two special tools used in the operation can be obtained they will reduce the risk of damage.

Under no circumstances should stiff bearings be loosened with oil. The immediate result will seem excellent, but bearings so treated will soon develop squeaks and eventually seize up completely. Once this has happened the substance of the bushing cloth will be transformed so that it can no longer provide a smooth surface over which the bearing pin can slide, and no amount of broaching will bring that surface back. Moreover the glue which secures it to the wood will eventually lose its grip, so that it comes away. And this is only the beginning of the catastrophe. Once the oil has got into the wood no new bushing can be glued to it, and any leather, cloth, or felt glued to any other part of it will also come away. A few carefree squirts with an oil-can may thus ruin an action for all time, so that the only thing to do with it is to throw it away.

10

STRINGS

The strings of a piano may be fixed in one of two ways:

(1) The far end of the string is bent back round the hitch pin and then twisted round itself a few turns to form an "eye". (See Fig. 13.)

(2) The far end of the string is bent, or "looped" round the hitch pin and then brought back to a second wrest pin, so that one string actually does duty for two. (See Fig. 14.)

To replace a broken string, first obtain a replacement string from the supplier.

Remove the wrest pin slowly and carefully. Too fast a movement may burnish the wood so that it loses its grip, and if the pin is not kept properly aligned the hole may be made oval.

If the far end of the string is to be held by an eye, bend the end round a metal rod of the same diameter as the hitch pin, and then twist it round the string a few turns.

Place the eye over the hitch pin, and thread the wire past the bridge pin and (in uprights) under the pressure bar or (in grands) through the stud, which forms the top bridge.

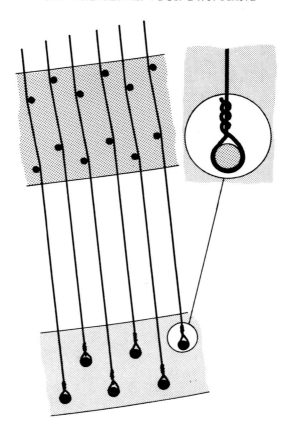

Fig. 13. An eye

Pull the wire as tight as possible, pass it over the palm of the left hand, and place the forefinger of that hand on top of the hole from which the wrest pin has been taken. With the hand in this position it is simple to measure off a length of wire beyond

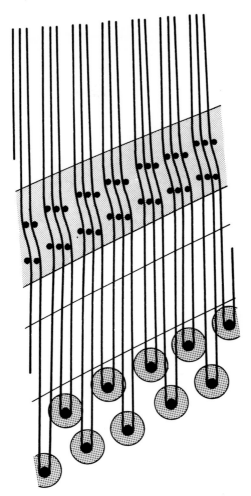

Fig. 14. Loops

the hole corresponding to the width of the 4 fingers of the hand. Cut the wire at this point.

Thread the wire through the hole in the wrest

pin, place the top of the pin in the socket of the tuning lever and turn it round until it has taken up enough wire to bring it level with the hole. Locate the bottom of the pin in the hole and tap it slightly with a hammer until it stands $\frac{1}{4}''$ above the other pins. Then turn the tuning lever to bring tension to the wire. As the pin rotates, lift the coil of wire from underneath with a screwdriver so as to bring the turns tightly together. Tap the top of the pin further down until it is level with the others, and bring the string up into tune.

If the far end of the string is to be looped round the hitch pin and brought back to a second wrest pin, follow the same procedure for the two wrest pins, except that the string only needs cutting once, and the tension on the two wrest pins must be kept roughly in balance.